ALTERNATOR
BOOKS™

MAKE AND UPLOAD YOUR OWN VIDEOS

KAREN LATCHANA KENNEY

Lerner Publications ◆ Minneapolis

Lerner Publications Company
A division of Lerner Publishing Group, Inc.
241 First Avenue North
Minneapolis, MN 55401 USA

For reading levels and more information, look up this title at
www.lernerbooks.com.

Library of Congress Cataloging-in-Publication Data

The Cataloging-in-Publication Data for *Make and Upload Your Own
Videos* is on file at the Library of Congress.
ISBN 978-1-5124-8340-6 (lib. bdg.)
ISBN 978-1-5124-8345-1 (EB pdf)

LC record available at https://lccn.loc.gov/2017002410

Manufactured in the United States of America
1-43342-33162-5/1/2017

CONTENTS

CREATE ON-SCREEN!

HAVE YOU EVER WANTED TO SHARE YOUR FAVORITE EASY-TO-MAKE INDIAN FOOD RECIPES? Maybe you'd like to record a solid skateboarding move or interview a neighbor. You can do all this by making videos!

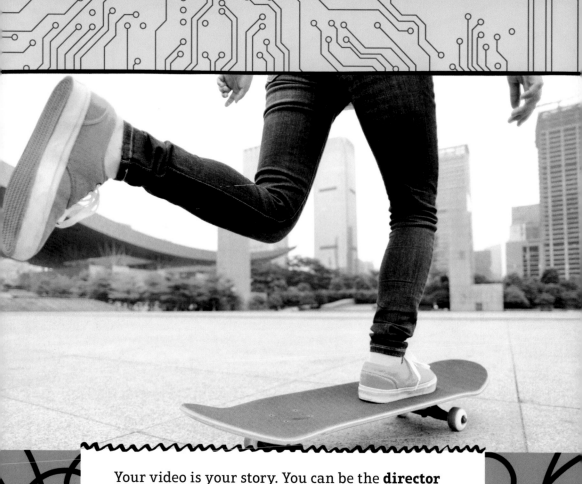

Your video is your story. You can be the **director** and even the star. What do you want to say? How do you want to say it? It starts with your ideas and some planning. Learn tips and tricks to make your videos more watchable. Then use cameras, phones, apps, and more to record. It might take practice to get the results you want, but hard work pays off—as amazing videos!

Edit and add **effects** to polish your creation, and then share it with friends, family, and even the public. Your story can reach others, teach them about you and your interests, and maybe inspire them to create on-screen too.

Are you ready to make videos? Great—LET'S CREATE!

CHAPTER I

READY TO RECORD?

SO YOU LOVE VIDEOS AND WANT TO MAKE YOUR OWN. Where do you begin? It starts with good ideas. Here's how to get those ideas rolling so you can start recording.

First, think about your passion. Do you love animals or helping others? Are you a people person? Are you fascinated by science? If you're passionate about something, it will show in your video. Brainstorm topics you care about and pick your focus.

Videos are a great way to capture step-by-step activities like science experiments. They let you see every step.

Do you know why you want to make a video? Videos can teach others how to do something, document an event, or tell a true or fictional story. Pick a topic area you like and know your video's intent. This will help you deliver a clear message.

Research videos online to see what you like. Here are a few video types to check out:

» **CRAFTING DIY VIDEOS** show step-by-step instructions to make crafts.

» **FAN VIDEOS** present thoughts from video makers on their favorite shows, movies, or book series.

» **INTERVIEW VIDEOS** show video makers asking questions of others to learn more about them.

» **TIME-LAPSE VIDEOS** are fast frame-by-frame images—they're fun for quickly showing how something's done.

» **VLOGS,** or video blogs, show video makers talking about their lives and interests.

You can show how to make beaded necklaces in a crafting video!

VIDEO TOOLS

IT'S TIME TO GATHER YOUR TOOLS. Besides video cameras, you can use phones, tablets, and computers for recording. A **tripod** helps steady a recording device so you can avoid shaky video shots. If you don't have recording equipment or a tripod, see if you can borrow what you need from your school. Some public libraries have equipment you can borrow too.

Video apps are great tools for shooting your video, but they are especially good for editing. Use them to put different shots together and add special effects. Some are free, but others aren't. Ask an adult for help finding and downloading a quality app.

Tripods come in many sizes, from so tiny that they fit on a tabletop to large enough that you need a truck to move them from shoot to shoot.

PEOPLE POWER

→ **DEPENDING ON THE KIND OF VIDEO YOU WANT TO SHOOT, YOU MIGHT NEED SOME EXTRA HELP.** Will you be using actors? Will you need to carry equipment to a **location**? Ask friends or family members if they want to help with your video. You can even include them in the **credits**!

A little preplanning with your moviemaking crew can help make sure the filming process goes smoothly.

Costume shops can be a great option for picking out clothing for your actors.

If you are using actors, how do you want them to dress? Will they need costumes or props? Look for inexpensive clothing or props at thrift stores, or raid your garage or basement for old items. Just get permission first!

CHAPTER 2

MAKING YOUR VIDEO

YOU'RE ABOUT TO BECOME A DIRECTOR, SO YOU ARE IN CHARGE. Part of being in charge is having a plan in place.

You might have just one shot in your video, especially if it's short. But many videos have several shots. A shot is a **scene**—one small part of a longer video. A video might open with a shot of a school. Then it might continue in a classroom inside the school, where the action occurs. It may wrap up with another shot of the school.

If you know where you want to shoot, the first step is to make sure it's OK. If it's inside a building, you might need permission from the owners. Next, make a script to outline your shots or sketch each shot in a **storyboard**. Once your location is set and your shots are planned, you're ready to film.

A professional illustrator made this storyboard, but you don't need to have top-notch drawing skills to sketch out your story. Rough sketches work just as well!

CREATIVE TIP

When should you shoot your shots? It might be easier to shoot the first and last scenes first if they're in the same location and then shoot any middle scenes last. Make a schedule, like the one below, and send it to everybody who's participating in the shoot.

» **10:00 a.m.:** front of school scene #1
» **10:30 a.m.:** front of school scene #3
» **11:00 a.m.:** classroom scene #2

Supplies needed:
-fake blood (corn syrup)
-newspaper
-costumes

Movie title: Attack of the Blob

Shoot at 12 p.m. at Tracy's

12 p.m.: Tracy's scene #1
1 p.m.: Bill's garage scene #2

Move to Bill's garage at 1 p.m.

A basic planner or even sticky notes or scratch paper is all you need to draft a filming schedule.

GET FILMING!

IT'S EASY TO MAKE A BAD VIDEO—IT'S DARK AND SHAKY, AND IT HAS SCENES THAT ARE WAY TOO LONG. A good video takes preparation and thought.

One sure giveaway that a video lacks quality is that it isn't steady. A shaky video is distracting. If you don't have a steady hand, use a tripod. This simple step will make your project look more professional.

Look through your camera's viewfinder. What's in focus? Is it the scene you imagined? You may need to move the camera, zoom in, or pan out. Check the lighting. Is it bright enough? Use extra lights, or move to a brighter spot, if needed.

Lighting can make or break a shot.

SHORT SHOTS

Watch a movie or show and time the shots. You'll see that many last between ten to twenty seconds. Short shots keep people interested. Each time the shot changes, the brain has to figure out what's going on. After about ten seconds, the brain has it figured out. Anything longer may become boring. So count to ten while you're shooting, and then . . . cut!

Short shots are one technique that helps hold the audience's attention in the film version of *Charlotte's Web*.

EDITING AND EFFECTS

WHEN FILMING'S DONE, YOUR VIDEO ISN'T FINISHED. It needs to be edited to make your video look much better. Use a video-editing program on your computer or a simple app. Cut the shots that you don't like—but you may want to keep some of the mistakes, called bloopers. They add a funny, human touch to videos.

You can also add some effects, like the sound of loud footsteps or a song you like. Titles, credits, and other text are graphics you can add, but use these sparingly as too much will clutter the screen and distract viewers.

Don't permanently erase anything that you film. The biggest mistakes sometimes make the funniest bloopers!

CHAPTER 3

SHARING YOUR VIDEO

YOUR VIDEO IS JUST THE WAY YOU WANT IT TO BE. What's next? Many sites let people upload and share videos online.

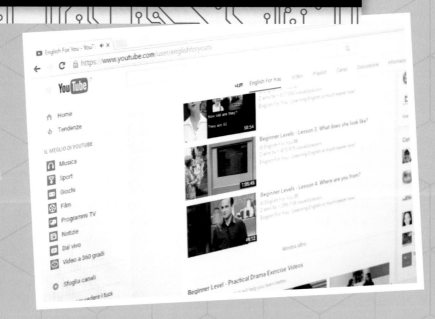

Check with a trusted adult before you share anything online.

Before sharing your video, get permission from a parent or guardian. Some sites have **age restrictions** on accounts. If you run into this, you could post on a parent's or guardian's account if it's OK with him or her—or you and your parent or guardian could create a shared account.

YouTube is probably the most well-known video hosting site. It lets you make your own channel, like a profile page. You can post many different videos on your channel. SchoolTube is a video site just for students and teachers. Students under the age of thirteen need approval from a teacher, parent, or guardian before their videos can appear on the site.

IN DEPTH

YOUTH FILM

FESTIVALS

Do you want to see your video on a big screen? A youth film festival might be fun to try. Look for community film festivals open to youth. Find out the **submission** rules and submit your video. If you are accepted into the festival, your video could be shown at a school, community center, or even a theater. You'll get to meet other young filmmakers and watch their videos too!

For young filmmakers like these, getting together with others who share their passion is an experience that can't be beat.

POSTING VIDEOS

IF THE SITE ALLOWS YOU TO HAVE A CHANNEL, PICK A FUN NAME FOR IT THAT DESCRIBES A BIT ABOUT YOURSELF. Also name your video with a good title. Sometimes the title alone will make viewers want to watch.

Write a description of your video's main idea, but don't give everything away. This is just a teaser, meant to attract viewers. Add tags too. Tags are words that are important to the topic of your video. For example, a video featuring funny shots of pets might include the tags *dogs, cats,* and *humor.* If your video is public and people type one of your tags into a search engine, they will be able to find your video and watch it.

Who doesn't love funny pet videos?

From creating elaborate scenes to setting up the most miniscule tripods, filming is a lot of work! Make sure others can find and view your masterpiece.

Maybe you've posted your video to multiple sites. List those sites in your video's description and provide links to the sites. Make posts on other social media sites including links to your video. New viewers may discover your video through another site.

MYA REYES

Meet Mya Reyes—one of the most popular kids on YouTube. Her channel, Full-Time Kid, is packed with fun, silly, and educational videos featuring her as the star. She shows viewers how to do science activities, dance moves, art projects, and recipes too. When Mya released a video about how to beatbox—making drum sounds with your mouth—it went viral. Mya's channel has had more than eighteen million views!

CHAPTER 4

STAYING SMART

THE INTERNET IS A PUBLIC PLACE WHERE CONTENT CAN LIVE FOR A VERY LONG TIME. Before you upload, think: Is your video's content something you want others to see? Does it contain personal information? You might not want everybody to be able to watch it.

ZACH ANNER

Before comedian Zach Anner became a famous YouTuber, he knew he wanted to be on-screen and make people laugh. He was born with cerebral palsy, a disease that affects body movement and muscle use. Zach's disorder stopped him from walking but not from achieving his filmmaking dreams. In 2010 he auditioned to have his own show on Oprah Winfrey's network and won. He now makes videos for his YouTube channel. His exercise videos, called "Workout Wednesday," have gone viral and gotten millions of views!

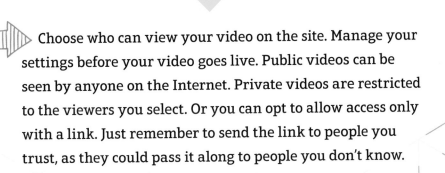

Choose who can view your video on the site. Manage your settings before your video goes live. Public videos can be seen by anyone on the Internet. Private videos are restricted to the viewers you select. Or you can opt to allow access only with a link. Just remember to send the link to people you trust, as they could pass it along to people you don't know.

TAKE THE GOOD WITH THE BAD

IF YOU ALLOW COMMENTS ON YOUR VIDEOS, BE PREPARED TO GET THEM! How do you deal with your comments? Acknowledge them with a reply and know that everyone has a different perspective. Some may not like your creation and that's OK. Take what advice you can, and use it however you choose.

Chloe x Halle is an R&B act made up of sisters and YouTube stars Chloe and Halle Bailey. Being in the spotlight can mean attracting both positive and negative attention, but Chloe and Halle take it all in stride.

CREATIVE TIP

You may not like everything about a person's video—but let's say you want to leave a comment on it anyway. What to do? When you write a comment, focus on what you did like. If you want to point out what you think could be improved, do so in a constructive way. Offer advice or propose solutions to the problems you see and try to stay positive. Remember, the video you watched is someone else's creation.

It's fun to be part of a **digital community** and support other video makers. View their videos and leave some feedback. You'll make them feel good, and maybe they'll comment on your videos too!

If you're ready to become a video maker, there's no better time than the present. You can express yourself in so many ways through videos. Have fun, stay smart, and be true to yourself. Then let your viewers see your art on-screen.

VIDEO CHECKLIST

ARE YOU ABOUT TO GET YOUR NEW VIDEO PROJECT GOING? Here's a list of the basic tasks you'll need to accomplish. Use it to make your video a success—from prep work to final upload!

1. Come up with a great idea! Think about your passions and interests. How can you make a video about them that people will want to watch?

2. Decide who you want your audience to be—other kids, your family, or the public.

3. Pick a video format you like. Will it be an interview, a DIY, or a funny story? Research videos to help you choose.

4. Get the equipment you need, such as a video camera or a tablet. See if you can borrow equipment from a school or library. Find video apps you can use for filming and editing.

5. Ask people for help if you need actors or assistance with filming.

6. Get props or costumes for your video, if needed.

7. Plan your shots, and make a script or a storyboard. Find locations for your video, and get permission to shoot. Then make a shooting schedule for the day you want to film.

8. It's the big day—film your video! Make adjustments while you film to get the best shots possible. You can choose the best ones and delete the bad ones later.

9. Edit your video, and add effects using apps or a simple video-editing program.

10. Find a site where you'd like to post and share your video. Get permission from a parent or guardian before opening an account on the site.

11. Upload your video, adding a title, tags, and description to the site.

12. Share your video with those you'd like to share it with. Use different sites to share links to your video. Then your video will get more views!

GLOSSARY

age restrictions: rules about the minimum age at which someone is allowed to do something

credits: a listing of the people who helped make a video that is shown at the beginning or end of the video

digital community: a virtual community in which users interact with one another online

director: the person in charge of making a movie, play, television program, or video

effects: the lighting, sounds, or scenery used to make a video or movie

location: where a video or movie is made, outside of a studio

scene: a part of a story, play, video, or movie

storyboard: a sequence of drawings that show the shots of a video

submission: the act of presenting a video for judgment by a panel of reviewers

tripod: a stand with three legs that people use to steady a camera or other video-recording equipment

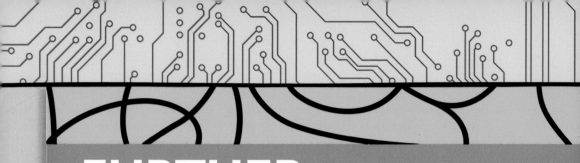

FURTHER INFORMATION

Common Sense Media: Essential Creativity Guide—Director
https://www.commonsensemedia.org/guide/essential-creativity
-guide/s/director/age%207-12

Kid's Vid
http://kidsvid.4teachers.org

Lindeen, Mary. *Digital Safety Smarts: Preventing Cyberbullying.*
Minneapolis: Lerner Publications, 2016.

Loh-Hagan, Virginia. *YouTube Channel.* Ann Arbor, MI: Cherry
Lake, 2016.

Mini Movie Makers
http://www.minimoviemakers.com

PBS: Full-Time Kid
http://www.pbs.org/show/full-time-kid

Pflugfelder, "Science Bob," and Steve Hockensmith. *Nick and
Tesla's Special Effects Spectacular: A Mystery with Animatronics, Alien
Makeup, Camera Gear, and Other Movie Magic You Can Make Yourself.*
Philadelphia: Quirk Books, 2015.

Pipe, Jim. *Make a Movie!* Mankato, MN: Arcturus, 2012.

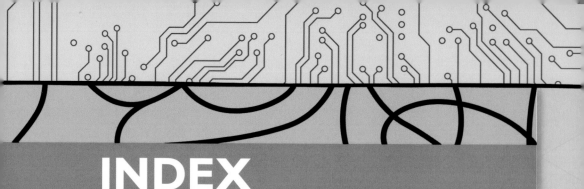

INDEX

PHOTO ACKNOWLEDGMENTS

The images in this book are used with the permission of: design elements: Iliveinoctober/Shutterstock.com; © iStockphoto.com/filborg; © iStockphoto.com/Sylverarts; © iStockphoto.com/chaluk; © iStockphoto.com/pixaroma; © iStockphoto.com/chekat; © iStockphoto.com/ulimi; © iStockphoto.com/slalomp; content: © iStockphoto.com/angelhell, p. 4; lzf/Shutterstock.com, p. 5; © Hero Images/Getty Images, p. 6; © iStockphoto.com/Georgijevic, p. 7; LanaSweet/Shutterstock.com, p. 8; © iStockphoto.com/tein79, p. 9; © iStockphoto.com/kali9, pp. 10, 17; bikeriderlondon/Shutterstock.com, p. 11; © iStockphoto.com/LuminaStock, p. 12; Mila Basenko/Shutterstock.com, p. 13; © iStockphoto.com/-slav-, p. 14; stockfotoart/Shutterstock.com, p. 15; © Snap Stills/REX/Shutterstock, p. 16; Stefano Garau/Shutterstock.com, p. 18; © iStockphoto.com/PeopleImages, p. 19; Jon Furniss/Newscom, p. 20; © iStockphoto.com/Alexakshas, p. 21; redsnapper/Alamy Stock Photo, p. 22; Courtesy of Mya Reyes, p. 23; © Tom Merton/Caiaimage/Getty Images, p. 24; WENN Ltd/Alamy Stock Photo, pp. 25, 26.

Front cover: © iStockphoto.com/vgajic.